BOATS

by Darlene R. Stille

Content Adviser: Steve Tadd, Discover Boating Program Manager,
National Marine Manufacturers Association
Reading Adviser: Dr. Linda D. Labbo,
Department of Reading Education, College of Education,
The University of Georgia

Compass Point Books

Minneapolis, Minnesota

Compass Point Books
3722 West 50th Street, #115
Minneapolis, MN 55410

Visit Compass Point Books on the Internet at *www.compasspointbooks.com* or e-mail your request to *custserv@compasspointbooks.com*

Photographs ©: Photo courtesy of Cobalt Boats/National Marine Manufacturers Association, cover;
DigitalVision, 1, 22; Mark Allen Stack/Tom Stack & Associates, 4; PhotoDisc, 6-7;
Neil Rabinowitz/Corbis, 8-9, 10-11; William B. Folsom, 12-13; AFP/Corbis, 14;
Jonathan Blair/Corbis, 16; Dave G. Houser/Corbis, 18; Nik Wheeler/Corbis, 20-21;
Photo courtesy of Houseboat Magazine and Houseboat Industry Association, 24; Gunter Marx
Photography/Corbis, 26.

Editors: E. Russell Primm, Emily Dolbear, and Pam Rosenberg
Photo Researcher: Svetlana Zhurkina
Photo Selector: Linda S. Koutris
Designer: Melissa Voda

Library of Congress Cataloging-in-Publication Data
Stille, Darlene R.
    Boats / by Darlene R. Stille.
      p. cm. — (Transportation)
    Summary: A simple introduction to various kinds of boats, including rowboats, sailboats, pontoons,
hydrofoils, steamboats and houseboats.
    Includes bibliographical references and index.
    ISBN 0-7565-0289-6 (hardcover)
      1. Boats and boating—Juvenile literature. 2. Ships—Juvenile literature. [1. Boats and boating.]
I. Title.
    VM150 .S875 2003
    623.8'2—dc21
                                   2002002950

Table of Contents

Boat Talk

Would you like to take a boat ride? Let's learn some boat words before we go.

All boats float on water. The part of the boat that floats is called the hull. Some boats have decks above the hull. You can sit on the deck. The front part of a boat is called the bow. The back of a boat is called the stern.

Now we're ready to try some boats. First, put on a life jacket. A life jacket will help you float if you fall in the water. Always wear a life jacket when you ride in a boat.

Row a Boat

Here's a rowboat. Climb in. A rowboat does not have a deck. Instead, it has seats that stretch from one side to the other.

Sit in the middle seat. Pull the oars through the water. Oars are long poles with wide, flat parts at one end. The oars are used to steer the rowboat through the water. They also move the boat forward or backward.

Sail a Sailboat

What makes a sailboat move? The wind fills the sails! The wind moves the sailboat.

The sails are pieces of cloth tied to a long pole. This is called a mast. On a boat, ropes are called lines. You use lines to move the sails up and down the mast.

You push or pull a stick called a tiller to turn a small boat. You turn big sailboats with a steering wheel.

Go Fast in a Motor Boat

You are in a motor boat, going fast. An **engine** makes a motor boat go. The engine may be inside the boat, or it may hang on the back.

The engine turns a **propeller** in the water. The propeller pushes the motor boat through the water.

Picnic on a Pontoon Boat

ISLAND RUNNER

PELICAN LANDING COMMUNITY ASSOCIATION

FL 2591 K

Pontoon boats are like rafts with motors. These boats float on metal tubes called pontoons. A flat deck sits on the pontoons.

You can walk around on the deck of a pontoon boat. You can sit in a chair or on a bench. You can even put a table on a pontoon boat and have a picnic.

Ride a Boat with Two Hulls

Some boats have two hulls. These boats are called catamarans. A deck goes across the hulls.

Catamarans come in a variety of sizes. Some catamarans have sails while others have motors.

"Fly" a Hydrofoil

Hydrofoils are boats that "fly" over the waves. A hydrofoil has wings in the water under the hull.

These wings work like airplane wings. They lift the hull up out of the water. You will have a smooth, fast ride on a hydrofoil.

Jet Through Water

A jet boat is like a jet plane. It has no propellers. Its engine shoots water out of the back of the boat. Water shooting out of the back makes the boat go forward. Jet boats do not need deep water.

Blow Along in an Airboat

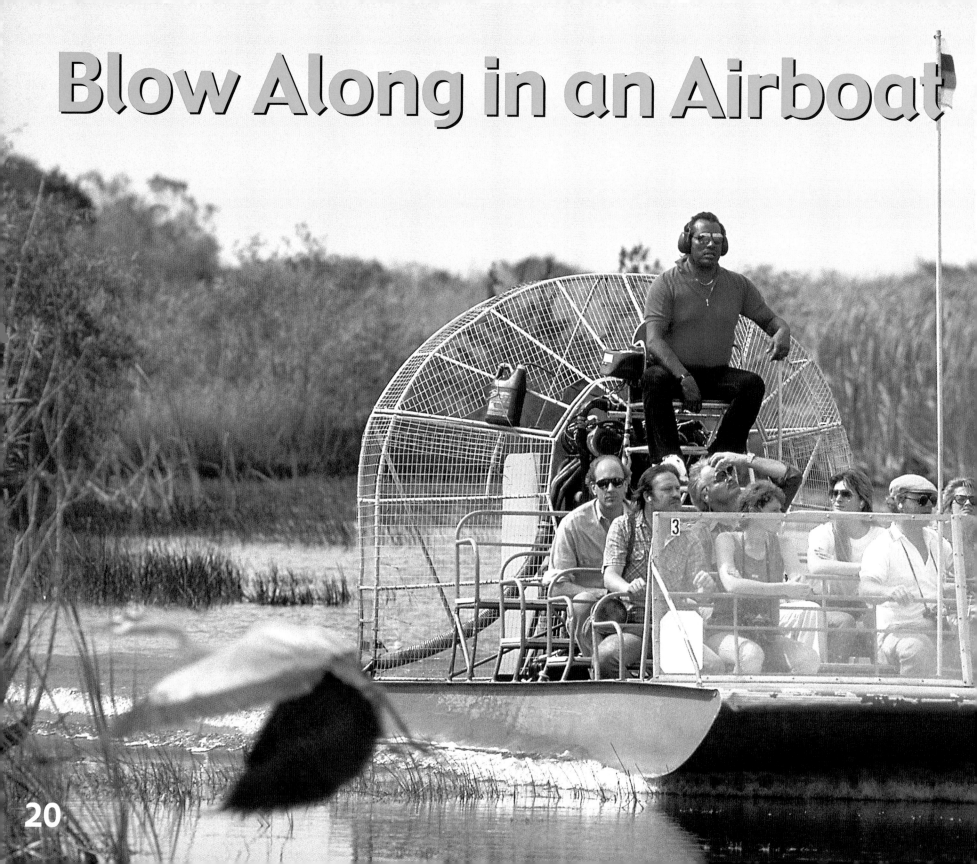

An airboat has a big fan on the back. The fan blows the boat through the water.

Most airboats have low, flat hulls. Airboats are good for getting around in a marsh or a swamp.

Travel by Steamboat

Steamboats have huge **paddle wheels** on their sides or on their stern. Steamboats burn wood, coal, or oil to turn hot water into **steam**. The steam makes the paddle wheels go around.

Long ago, people traveled by river on steamboats. Steamboats had rooms where people slept. You can still take an old-time steamboat trip on many rivers today.

Live on a Boat

You can even live on a houseboat! Houseboats have bedrooms called staterooms. They have bathrooms called heads. They have kitchens called galleys. Houseboats have living rooms, too.

Houseboats are usually used on small lakes or rivers. Big waves might tip a houseboat over.

Big sailboats and motor boats also have staterooms and heads. These boats are sometimes called cabin cruisers or yachts.

ferryboat

Use Boats for Play or Work

How can you have fun with boats? You can take rides. You can sail. You can water ski. You can even have boat races.

What kinds of boats can you use to do work? Tugboats pull larger ships in and out of harbors. You can use fishing boats to fish for food. Ferryboats carry cars and people across lakes and rivers. Coast Guard boats rescue any kind of boat that needs help. All these boats and many others can be used for work or play.

Glossary

decks—the floors of boats

engine—a machine that changes energy into a force that causes motion

marsh—soft, wet land

paddle wheels—wheels with flat boards attached that spin around and make a steamboat move

propeller—a set of rotating blades that provide enough force to move a vehicle

steam—water that has been heated to its boiling point

Did You Know?

Some of the first boats were called dugout canoes. People dug out the inside of a log to make a boat. First they set a fire in the log. Then they scraped the burned parts away until the log was hollow.

Ancient Egyptians made boats out of a water plant called papyrus. They tied the stems of papyrus plants together to make a hull. They sailed these boats on the Nile River. The Egyptians also used papyrus to make paper.

Steamboats were used as theaters long ago. These showboats traveled up and down the Mississippi River. When they stopped at a town, the townspeople came on board to enjoy the show.

Tugboats are so powerful that they can push or pull huge ocean liners. Tugboats also push barges along lakes or rivers. One little tugboat can push about forty barges hooked together. Their props can be as big as 9 feet (3 meters) tall. This is twice your height!

Want to Know More?

At the Library

Corey, Shana. *Boats*. New York: Random House, 2001.

McGrail, Sean. *Boats of the World: From the Stone Age to Medieval Times*.
New York: Oxford University, 2001.

Mitton, Tony. *Busy Boats*. New York: Kingfisher, 2002.

Walker, Pam. *Boat Rides*. Danbury, Conn.: Children's Press, 2000.

On the Web

Boat Safe Kids

http://www.boatsafe.com/kids

For fun activities and interesting information

Meet the Boating Safety Sidekicks

http://www.boatingsidekicks.com

To learn about boating safety, play games, and more

Steamboats and Paddlewheelers

http://www.steamboats.org/

For pictures of new and old steamboats along with sounds of their whistles and bells

Discover Boating

http://www.discoverboating.com
To ask questions of the "boat guy"

Through the Mail
United States Power Squadrons

P.O. Box 30423
Raleigh, NC 27622
To write for information about boat design, water sports, and other boating topics

On the Road
The Antique Boat Museum

750 Mary Street
Clayton, NY 13624
To see a wide range of antique boats

The Museum of Yachting

Fort Adams State Park
Newport, RI 02840
To learn about the history of yachting

Index

About the Author

Darlene R. Stille is a science editor and writer. She has lived in Chicago, Illinois, all her life. When she was in high school, she fell in love with science. While attending the University of Illinois, she discovered that she also enjoyed writing. Today she feels fortunate to have a career that allows her to pursue both her interests. Darlene R. Stille has written more than thirty books for young people.